GUERNSEY THROUGH THE LENS AGAIN

King George V and Queen Mary

GUERNSEY
through the lens again

including

Alderney, Sark, Herm and Jethou

Compiled by

VICTOR COYSH and CAREL TOMS

Phillimore

1982

Published by
PHILLIMORE & CO. LTD.,
London and Chichester

Head Office: Shopwyke Hall,
Chichester, Sussex, England

ISBN 0 85033 463 2

Printed and bound in Great Britain by
BILLING & SONS LIMITED
Guildford, London, Oxford, Worcester

CONTENTS

LIST OF ILLUSTRATIONS

INTRODUCTION

Published in 1978, *Guernsey Through the Lens*, in picture and story, dealt with the Guernsey Bailiwick from the inception of photography in the 1850s to 1914. Such was the popularity of that book that the authors, with the publisher's encouragement, decided to bring out a further album of photographs, complete with descriptive matter, covering the period from 1910 to 1940. It was felt that the slight overlap of four years would not matter; indeed, it would form a bridge between the two periods under review. The present book ends with the outbreak of war and the months preceding the German Occupation of the Channel Islands.

The format of the present volume differs slightly from its predecessor. It is unnecessary to trace again the history of photography in Guernsey, to dwell overmuch on our fortifications, communications of the past and on the origins of insular agriculture and horticulture. Avoidance of repetition is essential, even if the reader of this book is unfamiliar with the earlier one. We hope that islanders and other admirers of the Bailiwick will possess themselves with both volumes, thus ensuring that a pictorial record of island life from 1850 to 1940 will be theirs.

Again, we have felt the need to give Alderney, Sark and Herm their fair share of space, since changes have affected those islands as they have altered the face of Guernsey. It may prove rewarding to compare the local scene as it was in the past century with its appearance in the present one and in this respect development is a common factor in each Channel Island. For conditions before, during and after World War One were vastly different from the corresponding periods respecting its successor and, even had there been no such wars, the Bailiwick of Guernsey would not have stood still.

Since progress is inevitable, even if conflict hastens its pace, it is imperative to record these Islands' appearance and way of life as they used to be. Happily, the camera accomplishes this and, while the selection of pictures in this book are necessarily limited in number, it is felt they are sufficiently representative to provide readers with a taste of the past and to give those who come after a glimpse of this Bailiwick as it was during the first half of the present century.

Many of the illustrations come from the authors' own collections and, as in the first volume, we have tried to vary them as much as possible, so as to provide a portrait of Guernsey and her neighbours which will reveal life as it used to be. Once again islanders have been most co-operative in loaning their photographs for publication and special thanks are accorded to the following: Priaulx Library, Nos. 42, 64, 71, 133, 153, 155, 156, 159, 160, 173, 175, 176; States Ancient Monuments Committee, Nos. 2, 35, 203, 208; Mr. J. M. Beaumont, Seigneur of

Sark, Nos. 109, 185, 186, 187, 188, 189, 190; Guernsey Press, Nos. 3, 8, 14, 19, 20, 21, 24, 25, 26, 27, 28, 29, 30, 33, 37, 40, 43, 45, 46, 48, 49, 69, 103, 104, 114, 115, 116, 122, 123, 124, 126, 128, 137, 178, 181, 195, 196, 202, 205, 206; Miss P. Webb, No. 192; Mr. E. J. Hamel, No. 31; N. Grut Ltd., No. 80; K. McLeod Collection, No. 194; S. Cook Collection, No. 162; W. & E. Bailey, No. 163; and to Messrs Peter Button, A. S. Gould and B. E. H. Hassall for their help. Several illustrations in this book are from photographs taken by Thomas Bramley.

THE PLATES

CALM BEFORE THE STORM

King Edward VII died in 1910 and while he did not visit the Channel Islands as monarch he did so when his mother, Queen Victoria, came here in 1846, 1854 (on an Alderney visit) and 1859. Admittedly, he took no official part in the proceedings, being of tender years. His death plunged the Islands in mourning, which was relieved by the pageantry associated with the Proclamation of George V as King.

In 1910 cars were becoming rather less of a rarity than hitherto and a sign of the times was the arrival of Guernsey's first motor fire engine, named *Sarnia*, the supposed Roman name of the island. At that time the fire station was in Upland Road. In the same year the Platte Fougère lighthouse was completed and in itself it was an innovation, since it was operated from the shore by electricity and was unmanned.

During the visit of a squadron of Swedish warships a wreath was laid by their officers at the de Saumarez monument in Delancey Park. Admiral Sir James Saumarez had been stationed in the Baltic in the 19th century and his diplomacy won the admiration of the Swedes. Another rather unusual visitor was Dr. Charcot's steam barque *Pourquoi Pas?*, returning from the Antarctic after exploration work. At the same period a new local vessel appeared on the scene; the S.S. *Alert*. The ship previously bearing this name was christened *Serk*. They were employed as tugs and excursion steamers.

Seventy years ago life was placid in the Channel Islands. Our principal industries were the growing and export of produce—grapes, tomatoes and flowers—the quarrying and export of granite, and farming, in which cattle exports were important. Imports, so to speak, included visitors, for Guernsey by then was an established tourist resort, resulting in good shipping communications, several first-class hotels and local entertainments of a high order.

Visitors enjoyed the quietude of island life. They liked to stroll through the paved streets of St. Peter Port (as they still do), to wander 'down to the White Rock' and witness the movements of shipping. Perhaps they kept clear of the Old Harbour (now the Victoria Marina) when a collier was discharging, although the Albert Pier often provided the spectacle of the Sark boat's departure or the arrival of fishing craft with their catches.

Our guests could take the tram to St. Sampson's and observe the business of shipping granite or they could stroll through the quieter Delancey Park. Perhaps they caught the double-decked motor bus to L'Ancresse (this service had been inaugurated in 1909), there to enjoy a round of golf. On the common were prehistoric remains to examine and sheep to admire. Some of these pleasures remain, though the pace of life has inevitably increased.

A bus drawn by horses was a common sight in Guernsey early in the century. Services ran to St. Martin's, Cobo and occasionally further afield. Visitors also patronised the 'four-in-hands', chars-a-banc drawn by four horses and used in island tours. Passengers were perched on seats high above the hedges and their view, in consequence, was excellent. On the west coast (and elsewhere) sailing boats brought in catches of shellfish and these excited great admiration when they were displayed in the market. Today this is still the case, though the abundance is less apparent.

Another fascinating sight was the gathering of *vraic*, particularly on the west coast. Box-carts, each drawn by two big horses, hauled their loads of seaweed up the stone slipways and conveyed them to farms, where the *vraic* was used as a fertiliser. Other horse-drawn carriages, carts and delivery vehicles lent a more living aspect to the scene than motor transport, as did windmills at work, country folk in distinctive attire and the sound of Guernsey-French in town and rural areas. No roar of aircraft shattered the tune of birds and the sounds of animals in field or lane. One could walk on the highways and byways of Guernsey with a freedom absent today, while a bicycle ride was equally enjoyable. One was free from today's crowds, whether human or mechanical, and this proved as much a boon as the leisurely way of life we used to relish.

Island sport included cricket, football, tennis, golf and swimming. Sometimes there was horse-racing at L'Ancresse and yachting events were held, as well as regattas at St. Peter Port, Rocquaine and Grand Havre. Often there were sporting fixtures between the garrison and Militia, for at that time troops were stationed at Fort George and Castle Cornet. Militiamen received training at Les Beaucamps and on the King's birthday a great military parade at Fort George was the highlight of the year.

Entertainments took place in summer at Candie Gardens. Its bandstand was occupied by musicians on Sunday evenings and on weekdays by visiting concert parties. St. George's Hall was also an entertainment venue, like St. Julian's Theatre. The Guille-Allès Library helped to feed the mind, a task it shared with La Société Guernesiaise, the Guernsey Lecture Society and kindred bodies. While leisure was not overlooked, far longer working hours than those of today occupied much of the islander's day.

At times the unusual occurred. It is very rare for a Lieutenant-Governor of Guernsey to die in office, but this happened to Major-General R. Auld in February 1911. His military funeral was most impressive. In the cortège were garrison and Militia troops and thousands lined the route from St. Joseph's church to the Fort George cemetery. In utter contrast with that sombre occasion were the Coronation festivities later in the year. St. Peter Port's streets were lavishly decorated, as were other parts of the Bailiwick, and a spirit of loyal jubilation prevailed everywhere.

In those days it was not uncommon for mail steamers to come to grief— misfortunes not entirely unknown today!—and the stranding of the Weymouth packet *Roebuck* off Jersey, while it was spectacular, scarcely surprised islanders, even if it deprived them of a popular vessel for the time being. The building of lighthouses in Alderney and Sark in 1911 may have reassured them somewhat. The construction of steps at Petit Bôt bay proved a boon to those visiting the bay. The work was done in October.

A new lifeboat for St. Peter Port arrived in 1912. Named *Arthur Lionel*, she was of the 'pulling and sailing' type (that is, propelled by oars or canvas) and she was moored in the Pool off the Castle emplacement, where once the RNLI shed stood. The boat saw little active service.

The centenary of Sir Isaac Brock's death in 1812 was observed in St. Paul's Cathedral. Less impressive, maybe, was the discovery of Neolithic remains at Sandy Hook, L'Islet, later in the year. Far more sensational was the murder of an islander at Les Canus, St. Sampson's, the perpetrator of which was never discovered. The year ended with the commissioning of Mannez lighthouse, Alderney, whose beams shine forth near the wreck of the sailing ship *Liverpool*, lost in 1902.

Some events of importance occurred in 1913. On the recently-built Platte Fougère lighthouse a telephone was installed. More striking was a new peal of bells for the Town Church, in memory of its rector, the Rev. G. E. Lee. St. Sampson's church was also in the news when pre-Reformation relics were discovered hidden in its tower.

In former days it was a fairly common sight to observe large warships anchored off St. Peter Port and this happened in July, when the battleships *Prince of Wales*, *Bulwark* and *Venerable* paid us a visit. Possibly some of the ships' company patronised Guernsey's first motor excursion car, introduced at that time. The summer was somewhat marred by another local murder. Infinitely more agreeable was the visit of Winston Churchill, then First Lord of the Admiralty. A German cruise ship, the *Kronprinzessin Cecile*, was another noteworthy visitor. The year closed with the coming of Guernsey's first motor cycle—the precursor of a multitude!

The first of our mailsteamers to be fitted with wireless was the *Roebuck*. This was early in 1914. Soon afterwards another battleship, HMS *Superb*, arrived here. She was the first dreadnought to do so. A further remarkable visitor was the German cruising yacht, *Meteor*. English weights were introduced in the island in 1914 and another innovation was the sight of the eastern façade of the Town Church, revealed when a group of old inns were demolished. At the same time major alterations were made to the foot of Cornet Street.

Rain did not completely mar the celebrations held in July, when the statue of Victor Hugo was unveiled in Candie Gardens. The battleship *Russell* arrived for the occasion, French visitors were numerous, and there were fêtes and fireworks. These July festivities, as it happened, marked the end of an era. It was the drop of the curtain on the stage of peace.

1. A tranquil study of St Peter Port photographed by H. J. Singleton, long before the days of marinas! Guernsey-built fishing craft lie at their moorings on that still summer day, when canvas, rather than motors, propelled these little craft.

2. At low water St Sampson's harbour is almost dry and the two sailing vessels are therefore aground. Beyond is Mont Crevelt, with its Martello tower and battery. In the early years of the present century this northern Guernsey port was busy with vessels discharging coal and loading granite.

3. Berthed at St Sampson's is the sailing vessel *Zenith* purchased in 1908 by Capt. W. E. Loveridge and sold to a Scottish firm in 1918. She was typical of the coasters using that port in the transport of coal and stone to and from the island.

4. Fishing craft moored at St Sampson's harbour in 1913. These attractive sailing craft were locally built. Beyond them are steam and sailing vessels discharging coal. Later they will load stone.

Before the days of steam, communication between Guernsey and Sark was by ...ling cutter and one of these is illustrated. The *Alert* is seen leaving St Peter Port ...der power. She and her consorts remained in service until after the end of World ...ar I.

6. When the Great War broke out in 1914 one of our Southampton mail steamers, the *Vera*, was employed as a transport to take away the garrison, the Yorkshire Regiment, and the vessel is seen drawing away from her berth at St Peter Port, watched by many spectators.

7. (*left*) Harry Whales, a signalman who began work at the Spur signal station, White Rock, in 1914. As petty officer in H.M.S. *Castor*, he was severely wounded at the Battle of Jutland. He was usually to be found in the company of his dog, Mickey.

8. (*above*) Until 1940, ships approaching St Peter Port were signalled by means of flags and cones from a mast on the upper battlements of Castle Cornet. This photograph of about 1930 shows the signalman with his telescope outside his look-out, overlooking the harbour.

9. (*left*) On 3 October 1937 the auxiliary yawl *Reine d'Arvor* sailed from Guernsey to Australia with the Guernsey family of Mr and Mrs H. H. Brache and their three children, John, Noel and Anne. With them was photographer F. J. Woodwards. This French-built oyster boat arrived at Sydney at Christmas, 1939.

10. In 1930 the former liner's tender *Albert Edward* arrived at St Peter Port to become an excursion vessel. She was built at Southampton by Day & Summers, builders of the *Courier*, but was soon transformed into the motor vessel *Joybell III*, resulting in a complete change of appearance.

11. Leaving St Peter Port for Sark is *Joybell III*, the former *Albert Edward*. She was a very popular excursion craft which went into service in 1931 and remained in local waters until the eve of the German Occupation. *Joybell I*, a former RNLI life-boat, started running locally in 1925 and a larger craft, *Joybell II*, succeeded her until No. 3 came along.

12. In 1932 the battle cruiser *Hood* visited Guernsey, the largest warship to do so. She is seen in the roadstead and in the foreground is the handsome motor yacht *Bantam*, owned by the Rev. P. T. Mignot. In the right foreground is the sailing yacht *Rambler,* owned by Mr G. F. Peek.

13. A frequent visitor to Guernsey in the 1930s was the battleship *Nelson*, seen at anchor off St Peter Port with a pinnace speeding out of the pierheads. The warship frequently came here in time for the King's Birthday parade at Fort George, when Royal Marines and sailors joined the Royal Guernsey Militia in the ceremony.

14. Berthed at St Peter Port in 1938 was the steamer *Isle of Alderney* which traded between Guernsey and Poole for some years. She was formerly the *Devonia* and once regularly plied between Plymouth and the Channel Islands.

15. The SS *Courier* about to leave her St Peter Port berth for Alderney. Crowded aboard her are members of St Stephen's Church Lads' Brigade and Boy Scouts. Beyond the quayside spectators is a steam crane. The little steamer plied between the islands for many years.

16. (*above*) Guernsey's last 'pulling and sailing' RNL
life-boat, *Arthur Lionel* is seen under oars in the Old
Harbour of St Peter Port, watched by hundreds of
spectators. In that year she arrived on the Guernsey
station, but saw little action during her stay here.
Obviously, this scene depicts an exercise only.

17. (*left*) Packed with passengers, the motor life-
boat *Queen Victoria* was named at a ceremony at
St Peter Port in 1931, two years after her arrival. She
was Guernsey's first motor life-boat and served the
island for many years. The photograph was taken on
'Life-boat Day', 1934 and passengers were carried in
aid of the RNLI.

18. When the royal yacht *Victoria & Albert* anchored off St Peter Port in 1921, the local steamer *Courier* took excursionists around her. The yacht brought King George V and Queen Mary to Guernsey and several warships escorted her.

19. (*below*) In 1930 the steam coaster *Ravensdale* went ashore at Grand Havre and was later towed to St Sampson's harbour for repairs. She was acquired by the Guernsey Railway Co. Ltd., who owned her for a few years. She was typical of the type of steamer seen here 50 years ago.

20. The SS *New Fawn* entering harbour. Built in 1923, she traded between Guernsey, Poole and St Malo and replaced an earlier vessel, the *Fawn*. She carried passengers and cargo **and** often ran trips to Sark and Alderney. She left Guernsey in 1940 and did not return.

21. The motor yacht *Viking* built by E. A. Dorey, lying at St Sampson's harbour in 1933. Behind her is the careening hard and berthed nearby are the *Nith* and the *Stoneboat*. For some years these coasters were laid up there during a period when their services were not in demand.

22. What is now the Victoria Marina presented a very different picture in this photograph of about 1910. A steam collier is discharging at the quay and a sailing vessel is berthed at the Victoria Pier. While the background remains substantially the same, the use of the buildings has changed for the most part, like the harbour itself.

23. The triple-screw mail steamer *Sarnia* is seen leaving St Peter Port for Southampton not long before the outbreak of World War I. She was later torpedoed. A handsome vessel, she was the sister ship of the *Caesarea*, which survived the war and served the Islands long after it had ended.

24. (*top*) In 1939 the old steamer *Staffa* showed signs of sinking in St Peter Port harbour and the fire brigade was called to pump her out. The fire engine *Sarnia* is seen on the quayside. The ship plied between Guernsey an Alderney and during the Occupation she sank in Braye harbour and became a total loss.

25. (*above*) For about two years, the former mail steamer *Arpha* was a familiar sight in local waters, for she w used as an excursion ship between Guernsey, Alderney and Bournemouth. She is seen here berthed at the White Rock. In winter she was laid up at St Sampson's harbour. After the war she did not return to the island.

26.   Owned by Onesimus Dorey & Sons, Ltd., this Guernsey-registered steam collier, the *Portelet* (Capt. Alexander Walsh) is seen berthed at St Sampson's harbour at low water. She was blown up by a mine on the east coast of England in 1940. Years later another ship of that company bore her name.

27.   The building of the 'New' Jetty at St Peter Port began in July, 1926 and was completed three years later. In this photograph little had been constructed and ships continued to use the White Rock. In the picture are the *Roebuck* (*left*) and *Princess Ena*. Horse-drawn vehicles on the left have delivered tomatoes for export.

28. (*above*) The St Peter Port 'New' Jetty approaching completion. This was in 1929 and the first to use it was the mail steamer St Helier. Thereafter, mailboats ceased to use the White Rock berths and the Jetty, to some extent, also accommodated cargo vessels, as it still does.

29. The French steamer *Briseis* (3000 tons) struck Les Grunes reef, on Guernsey's west coast on 1 October 1937. She became a total loss, unlike her cargo of Algerian wine, which was washed ashore and eagerly sampled by islanders. Although 500 barrels reached the States bonded store, many more were broached by their finders.

30. The crew of the *Briseis* are seen rowing ashore at Grand Havre, following the sinking of their ship. Eye-witnesses stated that she seemed to tremble on her course before striking the rocks and disappearing in a great cascade of steam, smoke and water.

31. A Fairey F5 flying boat at St Peter Port near the stern of the Southampton mail steamer *Alberta*. The aircraft was in use in the 1920s and, like the mail packet, plied between Southampton and Guernsey.

32. The Sea Eagle amphibian has arrived at St Peter Port from Southampton, inaugurating the Imperial Airways service from Southampton. The pilot was Capt. C. H. Biard (in cockpit) and next to him was Sir Sefton Branker, Director-General of Civil Aviation.

33. The Weymouth mail steamer *St Helier* at St Peter Port in 1935, together with the Guernsey Airways seaplane, seen taxi-ing out of the harbour. its three engines were mounted on top of the wings.

34. St Sampson's Bridge viewed from the South Side in about 1910. In the foreground are mackerel drifters and across the harbour a sailing vessel is berthed near the patent mending slip. A tram waits at the terminus and traffic is noticeably sparse.

35. The mouth of St Sampson's harbour in 1938, when the stone crushing plant of W. Griffiths & Co. Ltd. was still standing. It was demolished during the German Occupation. At the quayside is the *London Queen*, loading stone.

36. The gathering of *vraic* (seaweed) was a familiar sight around Guernsey's flatter shores until comparatively recently and the photograph shows a box-cart laden with this fertiliser at the foot of a west coast slipway. The *vraic* was hauled from beach to farm, where it was spread on the land or dug into the soil.

INDUSTRY
AND
TRANSPORT

7. Before World War II the Northern Agricultural & Horticultural Society held its annual show and Battle of Flowers at Port Soif, moving to Saumarez Park later. The photograph shows Motor House Ltd's marquee at Port Soif in the 1930s.

38. This old Guernsey 'caravan' was built by Frederick Coysh, the Park Street coach-builder and this type of vehicle was in constant use in Guernsey until motor cars ousted it. The carriage is now at the folk museum, Saumarez Park, in company with other Guernsey-built vehicles.

39. Outside the Channel Islands Hotel on Glategny Esplanade are motor cars of the 1930s. The hotel is now known as the Savoy and the figures over the entrance have disappeared, like the balconies. The hotel's host, Wilfred Shirvell, was a great personality.

40. Guernsey's first motor fire engine was called *Sarnia* and is seen here at the fire station, formerly the Town Arsenal. The original station was in Upland Road. The appliance arrived in Guernsey in about 1910 and continued in use for many years.

41. This interesting and rare view of St Sampson's harbour shows it in its heyday, when thousands of tons of stone were exported. The photograph, dating from about 1912, shows the stone crushing mills on the North Side, with the adjacent cracking yards and those at the foot of the Vale Castle.

42. A victoria was an elegant type of carriage in the days before the first World War and the photograph shows it in all its dignity. A well-groomed horse is in charge of the liveried coachman, while a lady holds the reins. The passengers appear to be well wrapped up!

43. The Great Western Railway's cargo steamer *Sambur* entering St Peter Port from Weymouth. Built in 1925, she and her sister ship, the *Roebuck*, served the island for many years. Her accommodation for twelve passengers enabled one to travel overnight to England, a boon in the days before air travel.

44. One of Guernsey's many bus services in the 1920s was named 'Bluebird' and the picture shows the first 'Rio' to be used in place of the original Ford buses. The 'Bluebird' ran from St Peter Port to L'Ancresse via Bordeaux and its owners were Messrs Falla Brothers.

45. On 8 May 1939, mail was first sent by air from Guernsey and the photograph shows the Royal Mail van and the waiting aircraft. Present were the Lieut. Governor, the Bailiff and the Postmaster, as well as several spectators at La Villiaze airport.

46. (*top*) On 9 June 1934, the last tram operated in Guernsey and it is seen leaving the town terminus.
The service began with steam trams in 1879 and electric cars were introduced in 1892. No. 6 car ran from
St Peter Port to the 'tram sheds' at Hogue à la Perre only and soon afterwards the lines were removed
and motor buses replaced Guernsey's railway.

47. (*above*) The photograph shows a car leaving St Sampson's for St Peter Port. It is numbered 1 and
appears to be well patronised. Sailing ships in the background suggest that it was taken in about 1910.

48. Believed to have been Guernsey's oldest 'cabbie' in 1939, Mr George Watson is seen on the box of a 'chair' at Perchard's livery stables in Brock Road, St Peter Port. This type of vehicle was still to be seen just after World War II and a few survive in Sark today.

49. At Cambridge Park, St Peter Port, the last of Guernsey's steam rollers serves as a children's plaything. This photograph shows it still in use, and this ponderous appliance was a common sight on Guernsey roads for a century or more.

50. The art of making crabpots is still practised in Guernsey, although the use of willow has become rare, since wire pots find greater favour nowadays. Willow is imported from England and is expensive. The days when every fisherman made his own pots are over and the fishing industry itself is entirely different from what it used to be.

51. (*top*) In the shadow of the gasworks, at Les Banques, are the premises of the Fruit Export Co. Ltd., see here when trams passed them by, since the rails are visible in this photograph. The appearance of the buildings has changed since then, just as the lorry and the gas holder partly visible belong to yesterday.

52. (*above*) At Petit Bôt a water mill stood until the Germans destroyed it during the Occupation. The mill-house and wheel can be seen in this night photograph of the 1930s, when the building was a hotel and the area opposite was used as a beer garden.

53. Le Hêchet windmill stands near the top of the Ville au Roi and this photograph, taken in about 1915, shows the vanes intact. The tower still stands, having been ruinous for many years, and today it has been provided with a new cap and the careful restoration of the building enhances the landscape.

54. La Maison du Neuf Chemin, St Saviour's, photographed in 1938. When the valley was flooded after World War II, in order to make it a reservoir, this fine old building was submerged, like its neighbours. In times of severe drought the ruins are occasionally visible today.

55. Excavations started on the site of the dam of St Saviour's reservoir in October, 1938. This view from Les Annevilles looking across the valley and Rue à l'Or, shows the site cleared of trees. Extreme left is part of the old pumping station. In the house across the road are the offices of Pauling & Co. Ltd., the contractors. Work on the reservoir halted at the start of the Occupation.

56. This attractive piece of Guernsey countryside disappeared when St Saviour's reservoir caused the area to be flooded. The photograph, taken in 1938, shows part of the region which became submerged, causing the disappearance of several fine old buildings and farmland because of the pressing need for a better water supply.

57. This old reservoir at St Saviour's looks puny compared with the expanse of water in that area today. The reservoir can contain 240 million gallons of water and it presents an attractive picture in its wooded setting. On the right of this photograph is a granite pumping station which still survives.

58. The manufacture of iodine on Lihou Island was carried out early in the present century, when it was economical to make it from the abundant quantities of *vraic* (seaweed) to be taken from adjacent rocks and beaches. The photograph shows the plant and the large house which the Germans destroyed during the Occupation. In the foreground are wooden frames on which the *vraic* was dried.

59. Le Moulin de la Cantereine, at St Pierre du Bois, the last Guernsey water-mill to function. This photograph was taken in about 1935. The mill-house still stands in its secluded valley, but the wheel has gone. During the Occupation it was driven by an electric motor and corn was ground there.

60. The Vale Mill is still one of Guernsey's most striking landmarks, although it is less attractive today than it was when its sails turned in the wind. It stands on La Hougue du Moulin and was in working order until about 1914. The Germans used the tower as an observation post and added a storey to it, ruining its proportions, and unhappily it continues to lack the good looks it formerly enjoyed.

61. In the 1930s a branch of Lipton's grocery stores opened in High Street, St Peter Port and it continued in business until 1981. The photograph shows the staff grouped outside the shop in the 1930s. In the doorway is Mr F. Ephgrave, manager, and on the left is driver Mick Hamon. The cashier, Miss Toussaint, is wearing a dark dress.

62. The interior of Lipton's High Street shop reveals a layout and price range far removed from those of today. The photograph was taken about 50 years ago, soon after the premises were opened. Formerly they were occupied by Mr. R. Agnew, ironmonger.

A.D.1111.

63. Maitre Pierre Le Maître wearing a Guernsey smock. This miller of the north is believed to have been the last to have done so. This photograph dates from the 1930s. This fine old islander stands outside his home at Bordeaux, Vale, but although 'A.D. 1111' appears over the archway the building is less ancient than this.

64. In the last century cement was ground in a windmill at Le Mont Saint, St Saviour's. Its tower is seen in this photograph, probably taken in about 1910, when an unusual cap replaced the original and when the sails had been removed. Today the tower stands on its hilltop, now with a battlemented cap and whitewashed.

65. The fleet of vans owned by Le Riche's Stores seen on the South Esplanade in the 1930s. Three of the drivers are wearing long white coats and peaked caps, a uniform not to be seen today. Above are the houses of the Strand and Hauteville. These survive, unlike the glasshouses on the right-hand slope.

THE GREAT WAR

The Crimean and South African Wars had made relatively little impact in the lives of most Channel Islanders. True, some had fallen in South Africa, but life generally went on much as usual in the Bailiwick, since these conflicts were fought far from our shores. But the Great War, as it was called, brought the smell of the battlefield nearer home. There was fighting in France and in the Channel and to local historians it seemed that history was repeating itself.

On 4 August 1914, war-time measures were adopted. The Militia was mobilised and when the garrison was withdrawn (thereby revealing the Islands' lack of strategic importance) the local force became, for a time, our only defenders. Later, however, various units were in garrison, though for much of the war it was chiefly islanders who manned our meagre defences.

Watch was kept around our coasts, trenches were dug, restrictions were imposed. Several mail steamers became troopships and some were engaged in transferring island garrisons to England. Shipping services were curtailed, although inter-insular routes were maintained much as before. Mailboats were armed and later in the war merchant ships were camouflaged. Islanders saw little of the Royal Navy, but often French warships called at St. Peter Port.

In October 1914, 68 men volunteered for active service with the Militia, and 40 joined the Royal Irish Regiment. In the following March a Guernsey contingent left for training in Ireland and subsequent action in France. Meanwhile, the war was not being won and islanders, literally 'holding the fort', aroused the attention of the Lieutenant-Governor, General Sir Reginald Clare Hart, V.C., who felt the men were wasted here. In consequence, the States waived the islanders' traditional privilege of exemption from service overseas, save when the King himself required to be rescued from the foe.

The 1st (Service) Battalion of the Royal Guernsey Light Infantry was formed, the women of Guernsey provided its drums, bugles and company flags and in June 1917, the troops left for overseas service, their Colours having been laid up in the Town church. Later that year the R.G.L.I. fought at Cambrai, sustaining severe losses. War memorials throughout the island bear the names of hundreds who fell in that battle and elsewhere.

In Guernsey, meanwhile, a French seaplane base was established on the site of the Model Yacht Pond on the Castle Emplacement. The pond was demolished, a hangar was erected in its place, together with lesser buildings, and in 1917 a dozen small biplane flying boats became familiar sights in island skies and on the waters of St. Peter Port, as they taxied in and out of harbour. A crane hoisted them ashore when necessary.

The base was closed at the end of the war and in due course the site was cleared and the pond rebuilt. The aviators had been popular among islanders, especially at a time when strange faces were few. Austerity made life difficult and the absence of fit men caused the introduction of female labour. Women worked in offices, factories, on the trams and in other hitherto unusual circumstances. Rationing was introduced as supplies became scarce, thanks to U-boat activities and among their victims was the mail packet *Roebuck* and the cargo vessel *Guernsey*.

Islanders presented two motor ambulances for service in France and tobacco was sent to the troops regularly after processing at St. George's Hall. A military hospital was opened at Les Touillets, Castel. Peace was restored at the end of 1918, but rejoicings were tempered by the loss of many islanders as a result of a wave of deaths from Spanish influenza.

66. On the site of the old Ville au Roi estate a concentration of dwellings was built in 1933. Formerly fields occupied their sites and they formed part of the manorial property, whose house was suffered to remain, albeit ruinous, until ten years later.

ST PETER PORT

67. La Petite Ville, at the top of Ville au Roi, prior to its demolition in 1943. Once a most dignified and venerable place, it had fallen into disrepair when this 1940 photograph was taken, but many would have liked to have seen this medieval structure restored, since it was one of the most ancient in Guernsey.

68. St Peter Port under heavy snow makes a rare and lovely sight, as this picture reveals. It was taken in the 1930s from the vicinity of Clifton. Herm and Jethou also experienced the snow storm and the beauty of their contours was enhanced by the white blanket which enfolded them.

69. During the 1920s and 1930s much reconstruction work was carried out in the Bordage and this illustration shows demolition work in about 1932. In the background is Tower Hill. The street was narrow (as it still is), but in those days the degree of traffic was a great deal lighter than it is today.

70. Until about 1930 the Bordage was rather forbidding in aspect. Tall, gaunt stone buildings towered over the street and one of them is seen in its lower part. It was a warehouse owned by I. C. Fuzzey Ltd., who later demolished it to make way for their big store, known as Tudor House. Today this has disappeared and its replacement is less attractive, many considered.

71. The austerity of Bordage Street in the pre-1914 years is illustrated by this grim-looking picture. Lofty warehouses flank a muddy road surface and only a solitary pedestrian is to be seen. The severity of this St Peter Port thoroughfare was softened when many of the former buildings were replaced by others more attractive to the eye.

72. Where Woolworth's stands today was the *Victoria* Hote seen in this photograph of 1920. Originally it was called l'Hotel de l'Europe and Victor Hugo stayed there until he moved to Hauteville House. Opposite the hotel was James Mourant's gentlemen's outfitting shop, whose 'Jaeger Wear' advertisements can be seen.

73. (*below*) The People's Café just before it was razed in 1914. It was one of the old buildings which formerly stood on the quay, east of the parish church. The pillars and railings were attractive, like that part of the premises behind the granite drinking fountain. This remains, happily, like the Albert Statue beyond.

74. In 1914 some old buildings on the east side of the Town Church were demolished and this photograph shows the w in progress. They were chiefly inns and, while rather attractive, they certainly masked the beauty of the parish church.

75. Before the unveiling of the Island War Memorial in 1926 a small plantation occupied the site at the top of Smith Street. It is shown in this 1922 photograph, with gas lamps at either end and a stone wall flanked by trees. The Ford car is parked opposite St Paul's Methodist church.

76. A heavy snowfall is a rarity in Guernsey, so when this occured in the winter of 1935 photographers were busy. This picture shows St Julian's Avenue under a thick carpet and very little traffic is about. The snow on the tree trunk suggests that Guernsey had an easterly blizzard of some severity.

77. (*top*) A charming photograph of St Julian's Avenue when its borders were flanked by elms. These were felled in 1949 and their replacements lack the majesty of the original trees. Traffic, when this photograph was taken was extremely light and a solitary horse-drawn vehicle is using the Avenue. The railings on the left have been removed and so have the gas lamps.

78. (*above*) For many years the bandstand was a focal point in the Candie Gardens. Today a museum occupies its site, although much of the old building has been incorporated into the modern premises. The picture dates from about 1915, before a terrace was built on the east of the bandstand.

79. Smith Street in the days of World War I. Ford cars are seen outside the former offices of the *Evening Press* and a very pro-French atmosphere obviously prevails. The *Royal Yacht* Hotel in the background is now occupied by Boots and this firm also occupies the former premises of Hipps Ltd., men's outfitters.

80. Cornet Street as it was before drastic alterations made in the 1920s. Most of the buildings seen have been demolished and on the left of the picture stone walls and plantations now replace ancient houses. On the right is the pawnbrokers sign, which once adorned Lombardy House. The street lacks the quaint appearance of olden days, but it is much more hygienic!

81. Vauvert Street runs from Trinity Square to the foot of Victoria Road. This 1929 photograph depicts the St Peter Port parish refuse cart (a horse-drawn, two-wheeled vehicle, rather crudely covered), approaching Trinity Square. In the background is 'Mitchell's Corner', a popular clothing shop making the junction between Vauvert and Victoria Road.

82. (*above*) How very different is this photograph of the Town Church and its surroundings from today's prospect! The year of its taking was 1930, when a few buses used the Albert Pier as a terminus. Another was on the quay, just outside the church. An old hand crane stands beside the wharf and so little traffic exists that children can safely stroll along the almost deserted pier.

83. Fountain Street is still a picturesque thoroughfare of St Peter Port, but when its surface was paved and the original shopfronts existed the picture was even better. This old view, dating from about 1912, shows a complete absence of motor traffic and very few horse-drawn vehicles. In those days one could walk in the centre of the road with safety, something not to be done today.

84. Boxcarts, rather than motor lorries, were used during the building of Le Val des Terres in 1932. It was a great undertaking and as well as providing a useful entrance or exit to the town centre, work was found for the unemployed and a thing of beauty emerged on its completion.

85. The lower end of 'The New Road', soon to be renamed Le Val des Terres, after its official opening by the Prince of Wales in 1935. This photograph was taken three years earlier, when there was still much for the unemployed to do. The character of this valley has been preserved and the winding road is best appreciated by walking, rather than driving along it.

36. In 1932 unemployment in Guernsey was at a high level and to help alleviate it the Rev. P.T. Mignot gave the States a sufficient sum to enable some of the workless to build one of the island's most attractive roads. It is Le Val des Terres, running down from the Fort Road to La Vallette. Preparatory work is seen in this illustration.

87. The Albert Pier as it looked in about 1935. The tide is low and few craft are using the Old Harbour. On the pier are buses at their terminus. Today a large building stands on the pier, buses park at the South Esplanade and the Old Harbour has become a marina. Dozens of yachts are berthed there and the ancient character of the port has completely disappeared.

88. The Regal Cinema under construction in 1937. Later it was renamed Odeon and ceased to function in 1981. The building stands in Upland Road on the site of a nursery. The Strangers' Cemetery was formerly in the foreground of the photograph. The States now own the Odeon, whose future is uncertain at the present time.

89. (*top*) A martial display at St Peter Port harbour on the arrival of the new Lieutenant-Governor on 10 May 1911. He was Major-General Sir E. O. F. Hamilton and he resided at Saumarez Park in the absence abroad of Lord de Saumarez. The picture shows the band and guard of honour of the garrison, the Royal Irish Regiment, marching away from the Great Western Railway's berth, alongside which is the mailboat.

90. (*above*) Part of the Officers' Mess of the Royal Guernsey Militia, at the Town Arsenal, in 1930. Above the desk is a portrait of the Prince of Wales and below it is a side drum, formerly belonging to the Royal Sark Militia. Cases of accoutrements flank the portrait.

91. Firing a royal salute from Castle Cornet on the King's Birthday, 1914. The gunners are in full dress and the salute was of 21 guns. Today cannon still stand on the saluting battery but they are no longer fired, although a noon gun is fired elsewhere during the summer.

92. This 1914 picture shows the noon gun being fired at Castle Cornet. A gunner is spying at the Town Church clock to ensure accurate timing. The other man seems to be most improperly dressed, especially as he is being photographed! Another gun used to be fired from the castle at 9.30 pm.

93. On 1 June 1917, men of the 1st (Service) Battalion, the Royal Guernsey Light Infantry left Guernsey on active service. They left behind the regimental mascot, 'Joey', here seen at the White Rock with an admiring company of officers, troops and civilians.

94. Lieut. Col. R. W. Randall, A. D. C. (Militia) to the King, photographed in the full dress uniform of the Royal Guernsey Artillery (Militia) in the 1930s. He commanded this force for several years until it was disbanded in about 1930.

95. After the Great War medals were presented to members of the Royal Guernsey Light Infantry outside the Town Church on 29 February 1920. Also receiving medals were members of the Royal Field Artillery, including Sergt. Stanley Collins, who won the Military Medal.

96. This photograph of about 1925 shows troops of the Royal Guernsey Artillery (Militia) marching past the Bailiff of Guernsey, Sir Havilland de Sausmarez, at the King's Birthday Parade at Belvedere Field, Fort George. Other units of the garrison and Militia are seen in the background.

97. (*left*) Led by a French military band, troops are seen marching through Fort George on the way to the King's Birthday Parade of 1914. Between the mounted officers there appears to be a woman in white with folded arms. Legend declares that she was the spirit of France, making an appearance on the eve of war!

98. (*below*) Led by the mascot, Joey II (a Guernsey donkey), the band of the Royal Guernsey Militia, with troops in the rear, is seen leaving Belvedere Field, Fort George, at the conclusion of the King's Birthday Parade in 1935. Thousands always attended this colourful annual spectacle.

99. (*right*) Marching up the Bordage on a summer afternoon in 1935 is the Royal Guernsey Militia, led by its drums and band. They were returning from the annual training camp at Les Beaucamps, Castel, and the march through town was traditional and greatly enjoyed by all who witnessed it.

100. (*below*) Royal Engineers constructed this hangar inside the low walls of the Model Yacht Pond during World War I. It was for the use of French naval flying boats, established on the Castle Emplacement. These were the first aircraft to be seen in Guernsey.

101. (*right*) The Sherwood Foresters marching past at the King's Birthday Parade at Belvedere Field in 1936. They were in garrison at Fort George. Behind the regimental Colour is a party of men in old time uniform, adding a splash of colour to the troops' khaki.

102. Two smart young Militiamen are here seen in charge of Joey II, regimental mascot of the Royal Guernsey Militia in 1938. They were at Les Beaucamps during the annual training. Left is Herbert Le Poidevin and right is Maurice Le Heron.

103. Returning from service at the Castel parish church is the Royal Guernsey Militia, headed by the band. Their camp at Les Beaucamps was nearby. The photograph dates from 1935, five years before the force was disbanded on the eve of the German Occupation.

104. Men of the Royal Guernsey Light Infantry (Service Battalion) at the White Rock in 1917. They were about to leave for training in England and active service in France. Many fell at the Battle of Cambrai later that year.

105. When the R.G.L.I. sailed from Guernsey in 1917 they were seen off by a multitude of islanders. Here civilians and troops are seen en masse at the White Rock, while cab drivers look on. Many of those who left the island fell in battle later.

106. (*above*) After the battle of Cambrai in 1917 King George V visited the remnants of the Royal Guernsey Light Infantry. He is seen with President Poincarré and (*left*), General Sir Douglas Haig. Many islanders were killed in action at Cambrai and elsewhere and island war memorials bear testimony to the fact.

107. (*left*) During World War I Percy Le Ber, J. C. Guilbert, Eddy Dunn, Walter Mauger, Clifford Gaudion and Cecil Johns, of the Royal Guernsey Light Infantry, were made prisoners of war at Masnières and Cambrai on 1 December 1917. They are seen afterwards with a Belgian couple and their three children at Laeken, Brussels.

AFTERMATH

Early in 1919 survivors of the R.G.L.I. were given a great 'welcome home'. The States presented the British Government with £100,000 towards the cost of the war and later in the year a series of peace celebrations (including a Venetian fete in St. Peter Port harbour) restored the spirits of islanders. In November the first Two Minutes' Silence was observed.

The year 1920 was chiefly one of consolidation after the War's upheaval. The Island Police Force was formed, passports were abolished (as far as visits to and from the Islands were concerned), tourists arrived in increasing numbers and the mailboat services were fully restored. A newcomer was the *Lorina* and an absentee was the *Sarnia*, a war loss. The abolition of French money as our legal currency marked the close of the year, when the States formally assumed management of the public water supply.

Early in 1921 the Militias of Guernsey and Alderney were re-established on a peace-time basis. The garrison returned and amateur and professional troops turned out in force when King George V and Queen Mary, with Princess Mary, visited the Islands in July. They arrived in the royal yacht *Victoria and Albert* (with an escort of warships) and hot weather prevailed. The King and Queen visited Guernsey and Jersey only and their stay in each was brief. The Bailiff, Edward Ozanne, was knighted at St. George's Hall, a rare event.

The birth of the Guernsey Eisteddfod took place in November 1921, and at the year's end a new constitution for Sark came about. A month or so later Guernsey had its first 'wireless concert' and from then onwards the wonders of radio became more and more appreciated. Islanders 'listened in' with their crystal and valve sets and some evening entertainments suffered in consequence.

In 1922 the Guernsey Rotary Club was formed. A distinguished islander, Sir Havilland de Sausmarez, was appointed Bailiff, but otherwise nothing remarkable took place. The year 1923 was chiefly noteworthy for the inauguration of a flying boat service between Southampton and Guernsey. It took little more than an hour to cross the Channel and the aircraft taxied into St. Peter Port and moored to a buoy, whereupon passengers were brought ashore by launch. This was the start of regular air communication between England and Guernsey and flying boats continued to operate until the late 1920s, when the service temporarily ended. At that period there were 'patent mending slips' at St. Peter Port and St. Sampson's and in 1923 the Southampton cargo vessel *Ulrica* struck the Roustel rock and received initial repairs on the town slip.

Guernsey's first People's Deputies were elected States members in 1924. In that year the island voted £220,000 as an 'Imperial Contribution' to the Exchequer, something which aroused much controversy locally. The Chief Scout, Sir Robert Baden-Powell, came to the island in April and soon afterwards work on

'The Little Chapel' at Les Vauxbelets was started by one of the Brothers. In the autumn Miss Marie Randall, our first woman Deputy, took her seat in the States.

Early in 1925, after many years' service, the packet *Ibex* was withdrawn from the Weymouth run and the *Lynx*, originally a mail steamer and later a cargo vessel, was similarly withdrawn. She was replaced by a new *Roebuck*, which served the Islands for decades, like her sister, the *Sambur*. Another departure was the *Gazelle*, a vessel resembling the *Lynx*. The cargo steamer *Pembroke* remained in service for several more years.

In May, the Weymouth mailboat *St. Julien* made her first sailing to the Islands and a month later came her consort, the *St. Helier*. Both served us long and faithfully. Their contemporaries at that time were the *Alberta* and *Lorina*, with occasional help from the *Vera* and *Princess Ena*. The Southampton cargo vessels were the *Brittany* (later renamed *Aldershot*), *Ada* and *Bertha*. By then tomatoes were no longer shipped in wicker baskets but in 'chip' containers, made of box-wood, and much fewer grapes were exported than hitherto.

That spring, the Mignot Memorial Hospital, Alderney was transferred from its original site at the foot of Victoria Street to one opposite, formerly occupied by the *Victoria* Hotel. In August, Guernsey's first Stipendiary Magistrate was appointed: Mr. H. J. Casey.

The Island War Memorial was unveiled in January, 1926, by the Lieutenant-Governor, Major-General Sir Charles Sackville West (later Lord Sackville). Otherwise it was an uneventful year. The 2nd Battalion Queen's Own West Kent Regiment was in garrison in Guernsey and Alderney and in command of the R.G.L.I. was Lieut. Col. R. J. Leale. Commanding the Militia Artillery was Lieut. Col. R. W. Randall and the Royal Alderney Militia was commanded by Lieut. Col. W. R. Thompson.

Hauteville House, former home of Victor Hugo, was acquired by La Ville de Paris in 1927, in which year Mrs. Dudley Beaumont (née Collings) became Dame de Serk. In July a telephone service was established between Guernsey and Alderney and in the same month John Heyward swam from Guernsey to Sark in five hours. On a more sombre note, the States bought the Foulon Cemetery in November with the intention of building a crematorium there.

The British Treasury received from Guernsey a further contribution of £220,000 in January, 1928. Because the British Government declined to continue maintaining the Channel Islands' Militias, on the grounds of economy, training was suspended that summer. For the first time an aeroplane landed in Guernsey, at Fort George, and in August the flying boat service was resumed between Southampton and Guernsey.

Early in 1929 the Militia became news again when the States decided to maintain a reduced force. It was but a fraction of the former number and there were sufficient volunteers to avoid resorting to conscription. Its first commanding officer was Col. C. W. Carey.

In August the *Graf Zeppelin* flew over the island. Miss Muriel Woodward swam to Herm that summer and in October our first motor lifeboat, the *Queen Victoria*, arrived. The R.N.L.I. station was transferred from the Castle Emplacement to the White Rock. By this time work had started on the building of the New Jetty, necessary because of the increased size of vessels using St. Peter Port. The year 1929 closed with an innovation: 'talking pictures' and another less agreeable novelty: a crematorium.

108. Mr Winston Churchill, First Lord of the Admiralty, visited Guernsey in the summer of 1913, as this *Daily Mirror* photograph proves. He arrived in the Admiralty yacht *Enchantress* and is seen here with the Government Secretary, Col. J. Macartney. Later, Mr Churchill enjoyed a round of golf at L' Ancresse.

109. La Dame de Serk, Mrs Sibyl Hathaway, is seen here receiving a trophy for cattle, presented to her by the Prince of Wales during his visit to Guernsey in 1935. Sir Edward Broadbent, the Lieutenant-Governor, stands beside him.

110. (*right*) A floral archway was erected beside the commemorative stone when the Prince of Wales, in 1935, declared Le Val des Terres open. On the left is the Bailiff, Mr Victor Carey and beside the Prince is Mr R. Henry, stonemason. The stone's inscription is in French.

111. The Prince of Wales received many islanders at a garden party held at Government House during his Guernsey visit in 1935. Standing behind him is the Lieutenant-Governor, beside whom is his ADC., Capt. O. Priaulx. The Prince is talking to General Maude. Capt. Michael Carey stands beside the queue.

LE VAL DES TERN...
CETTE ROUTE A ÉTÉ INAUGUR...
SON ALTESSE ROYA...
LE PRINCE DE GALL...
LE 24 JUILLET 1935

112.   Edward, Prince of Wales, paid Guernsey a shor visit in 1935. On landing, accompanied by Sir Edwar Broadbent, Lieutenant-Governor, he inspected a gua of honour of Scouts at the White Rock.

113.   (*right*) King George V and Queen Mary on a very warm day in Guernsey. They were here in 1921 and the picture shows them with the Rev. George Whitley, behind whom is Sir Edward Ozanne, the newly-knighted Bailiff. The party is passing through lines of schoolchildren at Cambridge Park.

114.   A royal salute is fired from Castle Cornet as King George V and Queen Mary return to the *Victoria & Albert* after their visit to Guernsey in 1921. The royal barge is flying the royal standard forward and the white ensign aft. Oddly enough, the postcard from which the illustration is reproduced bears the casual caption, 'Castle Cornet, Guernsey'.

115. May, 1939, witnessed the departure of Sir Edward Broadbent, a much-loved Lieutenant-Governor. He is seen bidding farewell to members of the Royal Court, preparatory to boarding the mail steamer.

116. When George VI was proclaimed King in December, 1936, he was accorded three cheers by members of the Officers' Training Corps of Elizabeth College. They are seen outside the Royal Court House, where hundreds gathered to hear H.M. Sheriff read the proclamation.

117. When Edward VII was crowned King in 1901 St Peter Port's streets were loyally decorated. Here is Smith Street, gay with flags and bunting, with elegant ladies strolling down the hill beneath a device labelled 'Edward VII Rex. God Save the King'.

118. A flag-decked High Street made a colourful picture in 1911, when Guernsey was en fete at the Coronation of King George V. Old shop fronts flank the paved street and a small crowd poses for the photographer. Despite the June day overcoats are much in evidence.

119. In May, 1935, Mr Arthur Bell, Bailiff of Guernsey, died and his funeral at the Town Church was attended by a great many islanders. Even more watched in Church Square, where the horse-drawn hearse was followed by cars as the cortège moved off.

120. A solemn occasion in Smith Street, St Peter Port. It was the funeral cortège of the Rev. G. E. Lee, rector of the parish, who died in 1912. The horse-drawn hearse, escorted by clergy and choristers, is followed by a procession of carriages and many watch the sad scene.

121. Le Déhus dolmen, in the Vale parish, was restored in 1933 and among those in this picture are Mrs F. Ayscough (centre) who was the first to notice a face carved under one of its capstones. Others present were islanders who ceded this ancient monument to the States.

122. A film of Victor Hugo's novel, *The Toilers of the Sea,* was made in Guernsey and Sark in 1936, although lack of funds prevented its completion. Here the scene is set on St Sampson's breakwater and a reproduction of the *Durande* is approaching the harbour, watched by a crowd of 'extras'.

123. A general view of the Guernsey races, held at L'Ancresse Common in about 1936. Although it was normally a summer event, those attending are well wrapped up, although the weather did not deter a large number from attending this always popular meeting.

124. (*left*) Aquatic sports, arranged by the Guernsey Swimming Club in St Peter Port harbour on the occasion of the visit of HMS *Hood* in July, 1932. The old Great Western Railway's booking offices and refreshment room, seen in the background, were demolished in 1935.

125. A handsome Guernsey yacht, the *Rambler*, off St Sampson's harbour in 1936. She was owned by Mr G. F. Peek, a founder of the *Guernsey Evening Press* and a great island personality.

126. (*opposite above*) The Old Elizabethan Association dinner at Elizabeth College in 1938. This annual reunion is still held in the College Hall, traditional setting much appreciated by Old Boys and the staff of this ancient seat of learning.

127. (*opposite below*) The unveiling of Guernsey's Island War Memorial in 1926. The Lieutenant-Governor, Lord Sackville, performed the ceremony, which was attended by members of the Royal Court and States, Royal Guernsey Militia and a host of spectators. St Paul's Methodist Church forms the background.

128. Members of St Peter Port Douzaine at Fermain in 1932. The bay marks the boundary of that parish and the party is surveying the area on which public conveniences were built adjacent to the tearoom. In the background is a large house which was later demolished.

129. Guernsey welcomes visitors, but not his kind! In May, 1932, a whale was washed ashore at Grand Havre and the size of the animal can be gauged by the spectators. The whale's jaws have been kept open by means of a stake. Some years earlier a similar creature was washed up at Lihou land.

130. A States Meeting in the 1930s, when Mr Arthur Bell was Bailiff. On his right is the Lieutenant-Governor and on either hand are the Jurats (who no longer sit in the States). People's Deputies occupy other seats, like the rectors (left who are also members no longer. Since those days, the States Chamber has been considerably altered.

131. Assembled outside the feudal Court House of Fief Sausmarez are members of the Court in 1934. The two-storied building stands at the gates of Sausmarez Manor, St Martin's, and here official Court business was transacted under the presidency of the Seneschal, Mr Basil Rowswell (seated, centre).

132. (*below right*) In the porch of Anneville manor house, near Le Camp du Roi, it was traditional for the Court of Fief d'Anneville to transact its business. Since space was limited, several of those attending meetings were obliged to stand outside the building. The porch is the most ancient part of the house.

133. (*below*) Members of the Court of Fief Le Comte outside their Court House, at the gates of St George, Castel. Originally, the Court assembled in the chapel on the estate, but when it was demolished the present building was constructed, since it is an obligation that the owner of the property provide a place of assembly for the Court.

THE THIRTIES

This decade was one of significant change in the Guernsey Bailiwick. Transport developments, both internal and external, brought more visitors to the Islands and an increase in their populations, most of all in Guernsey. The old ships sailed away, newcomers were better in nearly every respect, sailing craft gave way to powered vessels, while ashore the horse was disappearing from island roads. Modern architecture gave an altered aspect to the scene. Radio, similarly, wrought a change of thought in islanders' minds. In short, the thirties were a link between the aftermath of the First World War and the prelude to the Second.

To begin with the ships, those vital connections with the outside world. Early in the decade came the Southern Railway's answer to the Great Western's 'Saints'. They were the splendid 'Isles'. The *Isle of Guernsey*, *Isle of Jersey* and *Isle of Sark* were efficient, fast, commodious and handsome. The old Southampton cargo boats were replaced by the *Haslemere*, *Ringwood*, *Fratton* and *Whitstable*, each of which provided accommodation for a dozen passengers.

This was especially convenient on days when no mail steamers ran, or when time was of the essence, since the freighters sailed at night and the Guernseyman could be in London the next morning. The completion of the Jetty coincided with the new ships' arrival. However, it reduced the size of the Pool and the palatial steam yachts which formerly anchored there (together with other vessels) were obliged to use the roadstead, unless they could secure berths in the harbour.

Local vessels also came and went in this decade. While the staunch old *Courier* continued to ply between Guernsey, Alderney and Sark, the paddle steamer *Helper* and the clipper-stemmed *Riduna* left the scene. Newcomers included the 'Joybells'—three of them, of various shapes and sizes—and later the big *Arpha* became an island-based steamer. So did the *Isle of Alderney*, formerly the Plymouth trader *Devonia*. The *Fawn*, on the St. Malo service, was replaced by the *New Fawn*, larger but less handsome.

In the early thirties, Guernsey Airways was formed and the concern became part of Guernsey & Jersey Airways. It used amphibians and the small aerodrome at L'Erée was employed. In 1936 the *Cloud of Iona* left Guernsey in poor visibility and crashed on Les Minquiers rocks, off Jersey, with the loss of all aboard. Flying, at that time, was a very different business from the sophisticated operation it is today and it is surprising that, in those early days, accidents were so few.

Road transport was changing, as indeed it was elsewhere. In the 1930s horses were still no rarities on the roads, for they drew the ponderous box-carts, laden with stone, coal or *vraic*, they hauled tomatoes to the harbour and many trades-men still employed them. Horse buses, however, had gone, although 'four-in-hands' and the occasional carriage were to be seen, as were horse-drawn hearses. The garrison used horses or mules for its transport, the officers (like those of the Militia) rode chargers, while on the farm the tractor was still something of a novelty.

Guernsey buses were legion. The trams ceased running in 1934, by which time the Guernsey Railway Company was already operating motor buses, which also replaced the trams. There were many private operators, too, whose somewhat primitive conveyances bore such fanciful names as 'Bluebird', 'Rapide', 'Robin', 'Lorina', 'Wayfarer', 'Paragon' and 'The Greys'. On a far bigger scale was Guernsey Motors, whose buses and excursion cars covered much of the island.

Bicycles were a popular form of transport, although the motor cycle (often complete with side-car) was becoming increasingly popular. So was the car. Despite Guernsey's small size, this vehicle has increased in popularity since the end of World War One and this applies in like measure to motorised commercial transport. The result is an island over-full of mechanical vehicles, a state of affairs which seems to have no limit. Today, the horse is rare on the roads, although a number of islanders possess carriages. Riding is extremely popular, though not on busy thoroughfares.

The 1930s witnessed a change in the old way of life which, during the Occupation, experienced a rebirth, albeit short-lived. Carts still carried *vraic* from beach to farm, though chemical fertilisers were gaining in popularity. Coal continued to be used in the home and vinery, despite an inclination by some growers to burn oil fuel. On the Castle Pier oil tanks were built and vessels discharged fuel on that rarely-used southern side of the harbour.

Timber was unloaded in the Albert Dock, now a marina. It was temporarily stacked on the South Esplanade, today's bus station. Half a century ago it was on the Albert Pier, although some vehicles took on passengers on the eastern side of the Town church. En route, buses stopped anywhere. Fares were low and cinema patrons were able to catch the 'picture bus', awaiting them outside after performances.

In Candie Gardens an auditorium was built and while it lacked good looks it was certainly a boon, since performances could be enjoyed under cover and, when the bandstand was enlarged, quite ambitious stage shows were presented. St. George's Hall continued to be used for exhibitions and dances, while cinema performances were screened at the Gaumont (formerly St. Julian's Hall), the Lyric (in New Street) and the North Cinema, near St. Sampson's Bridge. At the top of St. Julian's Avenue was 'The Palace of Varieties', a small theatre which also enjoyed other names. Dances at hotels and halls, sporting events within and without, swimming galas, regattas, horse-racing, motor cycle gymkhanas—these and other entertainments lent variety to island life. There are many who declare that in the 'thirties' Guernsey was a far better place in which to live or spend a holiday than it is today.

Nor was culture lacking. The Eisteddfod competitions proved extremely popular, concerts by the States of Guernsey orchestra were enjoyed, as were performances by the bands of the garrison and Militia. The Guernsey Lecture

Society was well patronised and so were theatrical presentations. The standard of local education was of a high order and many a young Guernsey lad or lass reached fame and fortune in consequence.

In the summer of 1930 the battleships *Nelson*, *Emperor of India* and *Marlborough* made a magnificent sight in the roadstead. H.M.S. *Nelson* was to pay several visits to Guernsey during that decade and her ship's company and marines often took part in the King's Birthday parade, a gesture especially welcome when we were without a garrison. The airship R100 passed over the island in June, at which time some of Castle Cornet's old cannon were removed. The year closed with the inauguration of a new telephone exchange in the Grange and a trunk line with England was established.

The year 1931 saw the transformation of St. Julian's Theatre into a cinema and the opening of the Lady Ozanne Maternity Home. Unemployment at that time was rife and a gift to the island of £2,500 by the Rev. P. T. Mignot enabled the States to assist the workless. He gave another £3,000 in 1932 and the unemployed were engaged in building Le Val des Terres, a new road running from the Fort Road to La Vallette, one of the most attractive in the island.

The Swedish cruiser *Fylgia* paid Guernsey a return visit in May, 1933 (the first was in 1910) and again her officers laid a wreath at the de Saumarez Memorial. This obelisk was destroyed by the Germans during the Occupation.

Those spacious days of the 'thirties' are illustrated in contemporary guides published by the Guernsey Chamber of Commerce, several of which carried a foreword by Compton Mackenzie. One could stay at the *Royal Hotel* for 17s. 6d. a day or at the *Channel Islands Hotel* for 12s. 6d. At the *Richmond* the daily charge was only 10s. 6d. By Southern Railway the return fare (first rail and saloon) from London was a mere 75s. A Polytechnic Guernsey holiday for a week cost £6 8s. 6d., including travel, seven nights' accommodation and three half-day excursions.

One could fly from London to Guernsey and back, via Alderney, for £4 19s. 6d. and from Southampton for £3. This was by Guernsey Airways. A return boat trip between St. Peter Port and Fermain cost a shilling. At about that time Bucktrout's 'Curly Tails' cigars were 45s. per hundred. As a point of interest, Fort Le Crocq, Vazon, served meals in the guardroom, courtyard and tower. Accommodation was available and a guide advertisement mentioned its moat, vault and battlements. The fort no longer exists.

Swimmers were in the news in 1933. Basil Rabey swam from Herm to Sark in 1 hour 53 minutes and John Heyward left Sark and reached Guernsey in 5¼ hours. Apart from these feats, the only remarkable happening was the building of the Ville au Roi housing estate in that year. The next was also relatively quiet, especially as Guernsey was without a garrison. Happily, this was restored in 1935, when the Sherwood Foresters were here. The year was made sad by the deaths of the Bailiff, Mr. A. W. Bell, the Rev. P. T. Mignot and Miss Edith Carey, the historian.

Mr. Victor Carey, the new Bailiff, welcomed the Prince of Wales (the future Edward VIII) when he paid Guernsey a brief visit. He opened Le Val des Terres, among other duties. On his accession to the throne in 1936, the customary ceremonies were enacted in the Islands and the late King's memorial was the playing fields at Les Blancs Bois. At the end of the year the old island journal, *La Gazette de Guernesey*, ceased publication. Currently read were the *Evening Press* and its rival, the *Star.*

The Regal cinema (later named Odeon) was opened in 1937, in which year St. Paul's Methodist church closed its doors. In the following year the *Hotel Beaulieu* (now the *Carlton*) commenced business. Saumarez Park, on the death of its owner, Lord de Saumarez, was purchased by the States, who re-opened the former St. Barnabas' church as the Lukis and Island Museum.

A large area of St. Saviour's was drastically transformed when the valley of Le Neuf Chemin was ultimately submerged, to be replaced by a reservoir holding 241 million gallons. Work began in 1937 and was completed after the Occupation, during which time operations were suspended.

Guernsey's airport at La Villiaze was opened in May, 1939 by Sir Kingsley Wood, Minister for Air. The shadow of war, however, rather clouded the rejoicings and in September the blow fell. On the 3rd, World War Two broke out, and its birth was the death of 20 years of peace.

134. Possibly Guernsey's first woman motor cyclist was Miss Edith Smith, here seen with her sister on a Raleigh machine purchased from Mr Gray, of Mill Street, in about 1921. Miss Smith was sister in charge of the Country Hospital (now the Castel Hospital) and her sister was matron. They were on its staff for over 21 years.

SOCIAL MATTERS

135. While Moulin Huet's rocks remain, such a beach scene is no longer to be enjoyed there. The photograph dates from about 1910 and reveals how (by modern standards) children were over-dressed when enjoying shrimping and other pleasures.

136. Today, how many men wear lounge suits and 'boaters' while paddling at Petit Bôt? Others in the picture are equally we wrapped up and they contrast strongly wi the attire (or lack of it) prevailing on our beaches nowadays.

137. Today, Guy Fawkes Day is still celebrated, but the elaborate processions are things of the past in Guernsey. Here is a group of islanders in fancy dress outside Sausmarez Mill, St Martin's, in 1935. The 'budloe' (Guernsey-French for Guy) looms above the party.

138. Fermain in the 1930s. Boats lie offshore and on the left is the landing stage for passengers travelling to and from St Peter Port. Today the scene is similar, although people don fewer clothes when relaxing on the beach.

139. Rocquaine Regatta is still well supported, as it was when this photograph was taken, perhaps 70 years ago. A typical west coast fishing boat, with passengers and crew, is seen at Portelet, with Fort Grey beyond. Sails, rather than motors, propelled such craft in those days.

140. (*above*) A group of golfers and friends at L'Ancresse in 1914. The youngest present was Victor Coysh seated in the centre. His parents stand behind him. The vast majority are wearing hats and favour more floral wear than prevails today.

141. (*below*) For many years an organ-grinder was a familiar figure in St Peter Port. Here he is, in about 1915, entertaining pinafored children and some adults in Church Square. An aspect of the photograph is its utter informality.

142. (*right*) Many of the photographs in this book were taken by Thomas Bramley, who had a studio at 'Hiawatha', a house facing the Gaumont cinema in St Julian's Avenue. A dapper little man, he was quickly on the scene when something of moment occurred and his camera also captured many island prospects which, but for him, might never have been enjoyed by posterity.

143. Off St Sampson's harbour a Guernsey-built fishing boat is seen under full sail. She is competing in the North Regatta, an entertainment still enjoyed by islanders and visitors every summer. The photograph dates from 1938.

144. (*above*) When the church of St Barnabas, on Tower Hill, ceased to be a place of worship it was used for a time as a soup kitchen. This photograph was taken in 1934 and shows the poor of the district seated at trestle tables. Many of them are children.

145. (*below*) For long *L'Erée* Hotel, on the west coast, has been a place of refreshment. In about 1912 it provided accommodation as well as meals and drinks for those enjoying that area. Today its appearance is vastly different from that presented above, although the main building still survives.

146. Les Caves de Bordeaux, in Upper Mansell Street, as it was before World War II. Then owned by the Feuillerat family, it was a place of great character, with a strong French influence and visitors delighted in the sight of the vast stock in the main bar and the mighty barrels seen on the right of the picture.

147. At the top of the Ville au Roi there used to be an inn, aptly called the *Traveller's Joy*. It stood there until 1933 when it was demolished to make way for a housing estate. It is seen here shortly before its long life ended. Beyond is the former Alexandra Nursing Home.

148. The splendid array of china at Les Duveaux Farm, St Sampson's. The vast dresser is flanked by a handsome long case clock. The house, owned by the Ogier family, and its remarkable kitchen are happily much as they were when this photograph was taken in the 1930s.

149. Les Duveaux Farm, in rural St Sampson's, has a grand chimney-piece in its dining room. It dates from 1604, although the house where it stands is of later date.

150. Edwardians at leisure in the reading room of the Guille-Allès Library. This handsome room (once part of our Assembly Rooms), remains, but the old bookcases, busts, hat stand and other Victorian features have been replaced by more contemporary fixtures.

151. Golf at L'Ancresse before World War I. Long skirts and plenty of clothing were popular, although one of the ladies was hatless. Then, as now, Martello towers were features of the links, but more dwellings cluster on the hilltop today.

152. An impromptu game of football outside the long-vanished waiting room and shop at Les Banques, St Sampson's. Made of corrugated iron, it was no beauty, but it provided rest and shelter for those about to board the tram. The picture was taken at the Half Way in 1925, and it would seem that the boys posed specially for the photographer's benefit.

AGRICULTURE

153. (*below*) Gathering seaweed on a west coast beach in the days when horses, rather than mechanical means, pulled their weight in Guernsey. Men are busy gathering the *vraic* before an incoming tide drives them ashore.

154. (*opposite above*) In the 1920s the export of cattle from Guernsey began to diminish, although it continued until the outbreak of war in 1939. Here animals are seen at the White Rock, awaiting shipment overseas. The fashions, steam and hand cranes and buildings are no longer to be seen at our vastly altered harbour.

155. (*opposite below*) While one works the other takes to the bottle! This pastoral scene, under the shadow of a church spire, shows a woman busy at her task while the male reclines with bottle raised. The horse patiently waits for his refreshment.

156. Haymaking in the good old fashioned way! This rural scene was photographically captured in about 1912, judging by the dress of the workers.

157. A plough drawn by horses and oxen was used communally by farmers when extra deep trenches were needed for parsnip planting. It was known as *La Grande Querrue* (the Big Plough). This arrangement was in use until about 1915.

158. Oxen, once upon a time, were used in ploughing on Guernsey farms. The animals, driven by a young man snatching a brief rest, were photographed before the Great War.

159. Horse-drawn vehicles made farming more attractive in appearance than do the powered appliances of today. This study of haymaking probably dates from the first decade of this century.

160. A straw rick in a Guernsey farmyard. Beside it is a water barrel, mounted on a horse-drawn vehicle. This scene could be almost dateless up to about 1920. The rick is raised above ground to discourage vermin and its top has been finished with artistry.

161. (*opposite*) Time for a spell! This old agricultural worker takes his ease in a wheelbarrow as he enjoys a rest and a bite to eat. This study was made more than half a century ago.

ALDERNEY, SARK, HERM AND JETHOU

Life in the smaller isles of the Bailiwick has always been something of a micro-cosm of that in Guernsey. There are, of course, significant differences, not only between the smaller and bigger islands, but in one from another. Moreover, since all are, to some degree, influenced by world events, what affects Guernsey to a large extent also affects the others.

However, Alderney, for the past hundred years, has presented a far more modern face to the world than has Sark. Ever since its breakwater and forts were built in the last century the presence of a garrison and of visiting warships has made its mark (literally so!) on what used to be a very remote place indeed. Sark, on the other hand, remains a feudal domain; a place where cars and aircraft, happily, are unknown, and even its tractors and hordes of visitors fail to shake the air of calm pervading the island. Even the Occupation, up to a point, made the least impact on Sark, compared with its neighbours. The very reverse was Alderney's fate.

Alderney

In 1910 and for many years afterwards, the steamer *Courier* sailed between Guernsey, Alderney and Cherbourg. She brought mails, passengers (often including troops) and cargo to the smaller island and sometimes conveyed cattle for export overseas. Government vessels used Braye harbour at times, like the ships of Trinity House. The Casquets lighthouse was served by the motor launch *Lita* and at the old jetty sailing vessels loaded stone, for the granite industry was Alderney's most important. Farming, fishing and catering for a handful of visitors constituted other mercantile activities.

The island's most prominent person was the Judge, who presided over its Court and States. In 1910 he was N. P. L. C. Barbenson, who was succeeded by Major R. W. Mellish in 1913. He held this position until 1938, when Brig. F. G. French became Judge. Members of the Court comprised six Jurats, H. M. Procureur, Prevot, Sergeant and Greffier. In the States sat the same persons, the Douzaine and, later, representatives of the community.

Cattle grazed on the Blaye (and elsewhere) and they made an attractive picture when they were led to the trough in Marais Square at the close of day. It was there that they assembled prior to walking down to the harbour for export. The town, indeed, wore a rural aspect, since many of its buildings were farm-houses. Between the paving stones grass often grew, so light was the traffic in the streets. Cars were scarce long after they were common elsewhere, though in the 'thirties' a motor bus service operated.

Alderney came to life on Sunday mornings (oddly enough) when the troops, resplendent in scarlet and blue, marched behind the band from Fort Albert to

St. Anne's church. Roman Catholics worshipped at their church at Crabby. This martial glory lent a dash of colour to the island scene and the troops' presence meant much to the islanders. They provided entertainment, sport and other social activities and must have given the population a sense of importance, entirely justified, since Alderney was still considered to be of military importance, perhaps more so than Guernsey was. For while the Royal Navy had little use for the port, whose breakwater had been built to transform it into a harbour of refuge, some of its forts, at least, were manned.

Thus in 1914 the guns of Fort Albert were ready to defend Alderney, searchlights were installed to cover the harbour approaches and the Royal Alderney Militia was mobilised. The *Courier* continued to serve the island and, although unarmed, she was painted grey. The island war memorial carries the names of 42 men of Alderney who were killed in the Great War on active service overseas.

In pre-war days there were about forty farms, most of them in the vicinity of St. Anne's. Reminders of earlier days were the windmills on the Blaye and the watermill inland from Platte Saline. Gravel was excavated nearby and its export is still important. Although most of the forts were in private hands, Fort Albert was still in commission, a military hospital was at Fort Essex and the Militia sometimes used Fort Tourgis.

Quarrying continued to be a most vital industry and the principal firm, the Channel Islands Granite Co., Ltd., leased the Admiralty railway for conveying stone from quarries to harbour. This stretch of line was originally laid during the building of the breakwater and it continued in use when great quantities of stone were tipped over its seaward side to protect the mole from the waves' violence. The main works were at Mannez, Battery quarry and York Hill, below Butes. The quarry and pier at La Cachalière (on the south coast) had been abandoned because of navigational perils offshore.

In the 1930s the hotels included *Scotts* (in Braye Road), *Belle Vue*, *Riou's* (Victoria Street), *Marais Hall*, *Victoria* and the *Grand*. There were several inns and guest-houses. The island school was in High Street (where the museum now stands) and at the Convent in Royal Connaught Square children were educated.

In January, 1936, the Proclamation of King Edward VIII took place in Alderney, watched by many. H.M. Sheriff, Mr. J. Pezet, read it at the Court House entrance and at Le Huret. The Judge, Procureur and Sheriff wore silk hats and Mr. Pezet carried his staff of office. Present were members of the Court, including Advocate R. L. Duplain, with P.C. Pike in attendance.

The peace of Alderney was by no means shattered by the opening of its airport in 1935. The pace of life continued as before and the island's special charm delighted those in quest of a quiet holiday. In the late '30s excursions were run from Bournemouth to Alderney by the steamer *Arpha*, as well as trips from Guernsey by the SS *Brittany* and SS *Courier*. Although islanders enjoyed reading *The Alderney Times* (a weekly), the Town Crier also informed them of what was happening. Another source of information then, as now, was the pubs.

Dances were held at the Assembly Rooms in Victoria Street, films were shown at the Rink, High Street, the Alderney Orchestra provided entertainment. Sport included golfing on the links near Fort Albert. Ormering could be indulged on Burhou and around the island's bays. If Alderney was somewhat isolated, if sea travel was at times an ordeal and if it was the least-known of the Channel Islands, Alderney was by no means stagnant. It enjoyed a life of its own and its very quietude was, to many, a boon.

Sark

Fundamental changes in this island are infrequent. Go there after 20 years' absence and not many alterations will be in evidence. Superficial developments occur, but in the main Sark life, even today, differs not a great deal from what it was half a century ago. The ancient calm, feudal atmosphere, natural beauty and indefinable charm appear to be oblivious to the clatter of tractors, the scores of bicycles and the noise of launches at the new harbour. The real Sark seems to be aloof to these superficialities.

In 1910 William Frederick Collings was Seigneur of Sark. He was a colourful, aggressive personality, ever ready to embark on the rampage and to pick a quarrel, especially with the vicar, the Rev. L. N. Seichan. The Seigneur's behaviour often landed him in trouble and made life difficult for his family. During his regime the old Godfrey home at Dixcart became *Stock's Hotel* and the Falle family house developed into Beauregard Boarding Establishment.

A stone jetty and steps were built at Havre Gosselin in 1912, making it easier for those landing there. The old ladder, at an uncomfortable angle for its user, remains, though few avail themselves of it. In the same year the lighthouse at Pointe Robert was constructed. Several fine houses were built by English settlers and others were modernised. The peace of Sark remained unruffled during World War One, in which 17 islanders died in battle, most of them serving in the R.G.L.I. The war memorial records their sacrifice.

Changes in local government were made when the Privy Council approved the Sark Reform Law of 1922, permitting 12 People's Deputies to sit in Chief Pleas. Five years later the Seigneur died and was succeeded by his daughter, Mrs. Sibyl Mary Beaumont, a widow. In 1929 she married American-born Robert Hathaway, who became Seigneur, though in name only. In the previous year the Island Hall was built—a great boon to islanders and visitors.

Artists have always found inspiration in Sark and in the 1930s those veterans, William Toplis and Ethel Cheesewright were joined by others, including Arthur Bradbury, Rowland Wheelwright and Mervyn Peake (who was also an author and wrote the Sark novel, *Mr. Pye*). Another island novelist, John Oxenham, wrote his last Sark book, *The Perilous Lovers*, a decade earlier. He died in England during the German Occupation.

In the years prior to the War Sark was well served with ships, including the *Courier*, *New Fawn* and the three 'Joybells'. Although no commercial flying was permitted (and this is still so), Sark sometimes received a visit by Lord Semphill in his own aircraft. He was a friend of La Dame, one of whose sons, Richard, also paid her flying visits. Another son, Lionel, made a film of Victor Hugo's *Toilers of the Sea*. This was in 1936 and much of it was filmed at Creux Harbour. However, it was unsuccessful financially and never appeared on the screen.

The Coronation of King George VI was in 1937 and Sark's celebrations included a royal salute, fired by its coastal artillery. In 1938 work began on the construction of La Maseline harbour, adjacent to Le Creux. It enjoys the advantage of accommodating vessels at any state of the tide, unlike its more comely neighbour. The undertaking was not completed until after the War, since work was suspended during the Occupation.

Herm

From 1889 until 1914 the German Prince Blücher von Wahlstatt was Tenant of Herm, then in the possession of the Crown. He introduced wallabies there and planted a great many trees around the mansion, then his home, which was described by Compton Mackenzie, a later Tenant, as 'perhaps the ugliest building in Europe'. The Prince and his family used St. Tugual's as their chapel, but normally attended mass at St. Joseph's, Guernsey, travelling there in their steam launch. On the outbreak of war the Prince was interned as an enemy alien and his steam yacht was laid up at St. Sampson's 'for the duration'.

During the war a small garrison was stationed in Herm, drawn from the South Staffordshire Regiment from Guernsey. The island was tenanted in 1920 by Mackenzie and he also rented Jethou from the Crown, to ensure not being overlooked. Both Herm and Jethou (under ficticious names) figure prominently in his novel, *Fairy Gold*. On sufferance from the Tenant, excursionists were permitted to visit the Shell Beach only twice a week. This was done for financial reasons, since Mackenzie had chosen Herm to enjoy privacy.

The cost of maintaining the place proved beyond his means and he sub-let it to Sir Percival Perry. Mackenzie moved across to Jethou, which was far less expensive to run. In 1925 there was a sub-branch of the St. Peter Port G.P.O. at the *Mermaid* Tavern, but it closed in 1938. Today, stamps bearing the Herm franking are of value to collectors.

Sir Percival made alterations to the little harbour by adding a concrete arm and slipway to the ancient pier. In 1933 he introduced a motor lorry and in that year the lock-up near the White House was used for the last time. The Tenant did not reside in the mansion, preferring the White House, although the mansion's ballroom was in regular use in winter. Perry remained in residence until the German Occupation.

Jethou

In 1910 its Tenant was Sir Austin Lee, who rented it from the Crown until 1918. For part of the tenancy it was sub-let to a Mr. Guy. During the Great War Jethou was in the hands of caretakers. Mackenzie lived there from 1920 to 1934. He did much to improve its beautiful garden and built an addition to the residence. It was a wing 80 feet long and 27 feet wide and in it were a suite of rooms; his library and vast collection of gramophone records.

An American, Harold Fortington, took over the lease in 1934 and he and his wife brought their car and chauffeur to Jethou. The Fortingtons built a garage, chauffeur's cottage, boat-house, reservoir and ramp during their stay, which ended in 1938. Thereafter, Jethou was tended by Mr. and Mrs. G. McDonald, who were caretakers for most of the Occupation, until the Germans ordered them to leave. Until after the war Jethou was not open to the public.

162. In the 1930s Alderney's airport was constructed and just prior to its completion the sands of Braye were used by amphibious aircraft. The *Cloud of Iona* is seen there, with the *Seaview* Hotel and the granite crusher beyond. This aircraft subsequently came to grief on Les Minquiers, with the loss of all aboard it.

ALDERNEY

163. Today Alderney's *Seaview* Hotel at Braye has an appearance different from that shown in this photograph of about 1930. The buildings opposite have also changed. However, the sands still tend to encroach on the houses' boundaries and small boats continue to repose beside Douglas Quay.

164. (*opposite above*) Victoria Street, Alderney, does not look so very different from this scene of about 1920, although the *Victoria* Hotel has been replaced by shops and the establishment so-named is on the opposite side of the street. Les Rocquettes House still faces the paved main street of St Anne's but, today, very few horses leave evidence of their present

165. (*opposite below*) A donkey cart pauses in Victoria Street, Alderney, a charming touch absent today. What is now *Georgian House* Hotel (on the left) was the *Commercial* Hotel, kept by F. Pike. The low building beside it remains, but the *Victoria Dining Rooms* (right) have long since disappeared.

166. Alderney's Court House and States Office as it appeared before World War II. Much of what was to be seen then remains visible, although the high railings and gas lamp belong to the past. The building is in what used to be styled New Street, but today it is known as Queen Elizabeth II Street.

167. The headquarters of the Salvation Army in High Street, Alderney, photographed in the 1920s. The building remains much as it did then, like the neighbouring houses. The boys of the island, however, wear rather different clothes today.

68. (*right*) It is interesting to note that when this photograph was taken the grocery business of D. S. Le Cocq was in Alderney's High Street, close to the *Campania pub*, outside which a man is standing. As usual, the photographer has his group of spectators.

69. (*below*) A horse awaits the farrier's attention at the smithy at Le Huret, Alderney. The picture must date from about 1920 and shows the *Old Corner pub* adjoining the blacksmith's shop. While there is no longer a gas lamp, the paving and buildings survive.

70. Little Street, Alderney, with many of its inhabitants in the picture. It must have been taken in the 1920s and shows one of St Anne's picturesque thoroughfares down which cattle were led from the Blaye to drink at the Marais Square trough.

171. Wrecks around Alderney were all too common until the building of the lighthouse at Mannez. In 1910 the steamer *Felix de Abasalo* broke her back on the Longis causeway and became a total loss. No lives were lost.

172. On 8 April 1912, the steamer *Rhenania* went ashore off Burhou and became a total loss. Alongside her is the Guernsey salvage vessel *Pioneer* and the ship's boats are alongside her. In the background are the cliffs of Alderney.

173. (*above*) A victim of the occupation of 1940 was the destruction of the cottage on Burhou by German Artillery on the Alderney cliffs, which used it as a target. Formerly a place of refuge and, for a while a residence, the ruins of the cottage survive near its replacement, a hut for bird-watchers.

174. (*below*) The rugged and wild appearance of Burhou is well seen in this pre-1940 photograph, which also shows the cottage, built in the last century. Puffins watch the fisherman in the foreground. They were more numerous then than they are today.

175. Judging by the scaffolding, Les Casquets lighthouse was undergoing work of some kind when this unusual photograph was taken in about 1920. Part of the yard and an isolated building appear, revealing the amount of space available to its keepers.

176. The fog signal at Les Casquets, photographed early in the 1920s. It was housed in one of its three towers, in each of which, originally, there was a light. Today, one powerful lighthouse suffices, although the towers remain and have their uses. On the left is part of the residential quarters.

177. As the people of Alderney left their homes in 1940 another, very different, party made their domicile there. They were gannets, who built nests on Les Etacs (the Garden Rocks) and the stack of Ortac. When the Alderney folk returned after the war they were delighted to see these handsome birds, who have continued to breed there ever since.

178. The Alderney Steam Packet Company's *Riduna* at Creux harbour, Sark in about 1934, soon after she had been acquired. Built as a Coastguard cruiser in 1905, she resembled a yacht. Her service in local waters did not last for long. Her name is said to have been the Roman name for Alderney.

179. The paddle steamer *Helper* off Creux harbour, Sark. Built in 1873, she was acquired by the Alderney Steam Packet Company in 1920 and plied between Guernsey and Sark until 1926, when she was badly damaged in a gale at Creux harbour. She was one of the last to use the St Peter Port patent mending slip and soon afterwards was disposed of.

180. Seining for sandeels outside Creux Harbour, with the Burons rocks in the distance. While two men draw in the heavy net another pair ensure the boat's stability. The boat was almost certainly built in Sark and the photograph was taken in about 1925.

181. The Sark regatta in 1925, with the Guernsey pilot boat *Surprise* lying second from the right alongside the quay. Crowds line the slipway and surroundings to watch a swimming event.

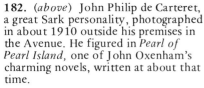

182. (*above*) John Philip de Carteret, a great Sark personality, photographed in about 1910 outside his premises in the Avenue. He figured in *Pearl of Pearl Island,* one of John Oxenham's charming novels, written at about that time.

183. (*above right*) Cottages at La Vauroque, Sark, which were demolished in the 1950s. In this picture, dating from 1910, their thatch enhances their appearance and certainly the dress of those gracing the roadway is a further attraction to a scene which Sark cannot offer today.

184. (*right*) The well at Beausejour, Sark, in about 1915. It is still there though perhaps it is rather less picturesque today. Old fashioned utensils include a milk can, a water can and what appears to be a wooden vessel. The woman's dress is also something out of the past.

185. On Brecqhou, off Sark's west coast, is a large, imposing house, with other buildings nearby. In 1910 only a thatched cottage and farm buildings were to be seen and these survived until the mansion was constructed in the 1930s.

186. Another view of Brecqhou's farm, photographed perhaps when Mr George Sharp lived there, after moving from Alderney in 1911. The cottage has lost its thatch, unfortunately, and corrugated iron takes its place.

187. Sark folk must have been startled at the appearance of a basking shark which became stranded at Port du Moulin in about 1933. The disposal of its carcass must have presented problems to La Dame de Serk, whose property it became.

188. Probably Sark's most uncommon visitor: a French naval flying boat, moored at Les Laches during the Great War. Craft like this were based at St Peter Port and helped in the hunt for German submarines in island waters. The photograph was taken in 1916.

89. In 1939 work began on constructing La Maseline Harbour, Sark, but the outbreak of war halted the work and it was not completed until after the German occupation. The photograph shows the construction of a tunnel through the rock face and the tracks of a light railway used in the operations.

90. The wooden bridge which used to link the great rock known as the Moie de Mouton with Sark's west coast. It was photographed in about 1915, it was a well-built piece of work, although persuading sheep to scale the ladder at its extremity must have presented problems. Ultimately the bridge became unsafe and it was demolished.

191. The main entrance to La Seigneurie when wooden gates spanned the archway. They were replaced by handsome iron gates on the marriage of La Dame de Serk and Mr. R.W. Hathaway by the people of Sark in 1929 — a handsome gift indeed.

Seigneurie Gateway, Sark.

192. *Sark's Stocks* Hotel looked even more attractive in the days when its main building was thatched. The photograph was taken in about 1910, before it was a hotel and when the Godfrey family resided there.

93. Berthed at Creux harbour are the *Courier* and *Joybell III* (in the pierheads). There was a time when these were rivals and in the 1930s fares were cut to a ridiculously low level in an effort to eliminate one of the two competing companies. Ultimately Sark Motorships acquired the Alderney Steam Packet Company, owners of the *Courier*.

194. Herm has hosted many unusual visitors, but none more rare than members of the Officers' Training Corps of Elizabeth College, seen on its peir in about 1930. They were there on a training exercise.

195. (*below*) Members of La Société Guernesiaise in the garden of Jethou's residence in 1931. They travelled there from Guernsey in the launch, *Isle of Herm* and it came on to rain during their stay, as open umbrellas reveal. The excursion, however, was most successful.

196. (*opposite above*) The SS *Courier* at anchor off Rosière steps. Herm, the low water landing place. The photograph dates from the early 1920s and shows passengers descending the steps in order to board the boat approaching ther from the ship. In those days landing at Herm was restricted, since its tenant, Compton Mackenzie, tolerated visitors only because of the revenue they produced.

197. (*opposite below*) The Mermaid cottages, Herm, in the 1920s. In some respects they still appear as they used to be, although they are now flanked by shops on one side and, in summer, an extremely busy *Mermaid* pub and restuaran on the other.

198. *(above)* Someone spelt out 'Herm, C. I.' in shells taken from the adjoining Shell Beach, one of Herm's most popular resorts. The photographer was there early in the 1920s, when visitors were few. Those who did go there were restricted to this beach and the path from the harbour leading to it. Belvoir bay beyond was out of bounds to tourists.

199. *(right)* Herm, earlier this century, presented a rather more bare appearance than it does today, for this photograph shows the beginning of the hill road devoid of the trees now growing there. Gone are the gates shown in the picture, although the stone pillars remain. Gone also, no doubt, are those grouped beside them.

200. *(left)* In about 1910 Jethou was leased from the Crown by Sir Austin Lee. During his tenancy Mr Richard Brian Le Page was in charge and the only link the island had with Guernsey was a 15 ft sailing boat, the *Dauntless.* Also living in Jethou then were (left to right) Elsie Moitie, Mrs Ivey Martel, Walter Moitie, M Le Page, Miss Trephina La Page, baby Florence Moitie and Miss Maud Cummings.

PRELUDE TO DISASTER

Surely no islander ever imagined that World War Two would make a lasting impression on him. True, on its outbreak on 3 September 1939, certain precautions were taken, such as painting local steamers grey, observing the black-out and the curtailment of shipping and air services. The garrison left and the Militia, mobilised for training earlier than usual, became the island's sole defence, but not for one moment did anyone suppose it would be needed. As in the previous war, it was assumed that the Islands would be immune from attack (of what strategic use were they?) and, as the quiet war proceeded, it was thought that Guernsey would prove ideal as a holiday resort 'away from it all'.

Militia guards were posted at the airport, Fort Doyle (where a telephone cable was) and at Saints (where there was another). Guards were also mounted at the fuel tanks in Bulwer Avenue and at the Castle emplacement. When the R.A.F. occupied the airport it provided its own guards. Some Militiamen were sent to Alderney when a machine gun training centre was established there. Because of the times of mailboat arrivals, the Sunday newspapers were brought over by the *New Fawn* on her Saturday night sailing from Poole.

Rationing of petrol, butter, bacon, ham and sugar began at the same time as in Britain. Many islanders did much work for the Red Cross, to which they subscribed generously. As the war progressed, a modified air service was operated and the mailboats left the island at night, sailing to Southampton only. The Poole service was abandoned.

Critics declared that the black-out was useless, since the island's shape was clearly visible at night by aircraft, thanks to the line of white surf around its seaboard. Gulls on the airport were shot and fishing was permitted on Sundays. Life was still reasonably normal. From time to time troops were stationed in Guernsey and Alderney.

In February 1940, the Island Defence Force replaced the Militia. Its formation was agreed by the States when it was realised that Militiamen would be better employed serving in the Army overseas rather than at Les Beaucamps. The I.D.F. comprised a hundred veterans wearing Militia uniform. For the most part, Militiamen joined the Royal Artillery and the Hampshire Regiment.

Meanwhile, the R.A.F. based some flying boats at St. Peter Port, other aircraft shared the airport with civilian machines and several huts for R.A.F. use were built there. Neighbouring hotels also accommodated R.A.F. personnel. By April about 300 airmen were stationed in the island and some 40 bombers were parked at La Villiaze, close to the road. In High Street were a canteen and rest room for servicemen.

In June, the Lieutenant-Governor, Major-General A. P. D. Telpher Smollett, was replaced by Major-General J. R. Minshull Ford. The swearing-in ceremony at the Royal Court was briefer than usual and equally short was his term of office. At Whitsun conditions were still sufficiently normal for the *New Fawn* to operate a well-supported excursion to Alderney.

Nevertheless, the military situation was beginning to deteriorate on the continent. A body of Local Defence Volunteers was formed, drawn chiefly from the British Legion and air rifle clubs, and armed guards were posted at vulnerable points. Signposts were removed from the countryside and a feeling of unease prevailed throughout the Bailiwick. The arrival of boatloads of French refugees in Alderney and Sark was, in effect, a prelude to the Occupation. The evacuation of troops, schoolchildren and others followed. Guernsey and Jersey were subjected to savage air raids and the illusion that they were free from invasion was shattered.

In the summer of 1940 a flight of gannets settled on Ortac and Les Etacs, great rocks off the shores of Alderney. At the same time the people of that island sailed away on the eve of its occupation by the enemy. Is it too fanciful to suggest that while evil stepped ashore on Alderney's soil goodness took wing and alighted nearby? In God's good time the foe departed, but the gracious birds remained and, when the folk of Alderney came home again the splendour of the gannets was theirs, perhaps for all time.

Of the German Occupation this book has nothing to say. Much has been written of this, perhaps the most poignant chapter in Channel Islands' history. Signs of those unhappy years are not wanting and one reason for this volume is to place on record some of our island features which the Occupation either radically changed or completely destroyed. The coming of peace in 1945 opened a fresh epoch in the Islands' life and post-war developments wrought yet more changes on the face of the Bailiwick.

MISCELLANEOUS

201. The de Saumarez Memorial in Delancey Park before its destruction by the Germans during the occupation. The obelisk commemorated Guernsey's Admiral Lord de Saumarez and around the base of the column were bronze plaques (preserved at Castle Cornet), depicting a bust of the Admiral, some of his naval triumphs and one showing his action off Guernsey in 1794.

202. The observatory at the rear of Lukis House, Grange photographed probably in 1921, when work on the building was completed. It was used for meteorological purposes for some years. The picture shows the garden of Lukis House, now a car park and, beyond, is Victoria Tower.

203. Frère Déodat at work on his creation, the celebrated 'Little Chapel' at Les Vauxbelets, St Andrew's, the Mecca of countless visitors to Guernsey. It was started in 1914 and the grotto was finished within a few months. Subsequently it was greatly enlarged, thanks to innumerable pieces of pottery and broken china used in its construction and presented by well-wishers.

204. The special interest in this illustration of Fermain bay is the large building seen behind the Martello tower. It was the annexe of *Le Chalet* Hotel and it was standing in 1936, the date of this photograph. Later it was demolished (happily), but the foundations survive.

205. Box-carts, once so common in Guernsey, are museum pieces today. Here are several, complete with horses in their best harness, seen at a cattle show in the 1930s. The judges are deciding which is the best of the exhibits.

6. Unadopted roads were once common in ~~Gu~~ernsey and one of them has its distinctive ~~no~~tice board well shown in this 1923 photograph. ~~It~~ was soon after this year that some of these ~~rou~~gh-surfaced roads were adopted by the States, ~~wh~~en their condition improved.

7. (*below*) Le Variouf, as it used to be before ~~Wo~~rld War II. The charm of this hillside hamlet ~~ab~~ove Petit Bôt is still there, but somehow its ~~mo~~re ancient appearance was more attractive.

8. In 1913 Guernsey's postmen po- for this photograph. They are wear- the uniform of the G.P.O. for it was ~~not~~ until 1969 that Guernsey assumed ~~con~~trol of the Bailiwick postal services ~~and~~ a distinctive uniform was devised.

209. Conger fishing in Guernsey. Two very fine fish are held aloft by the triumphant anglers, neither of whom is wearing the kind of clothing worn by fishermen of today. This photograph of the 1930s was taken in a creek on the south coast.